COMRADES IN CHRIST

GEORGE E. VANDEMAN

Pacific Press Publishing Association
Boise, Idaho
Oshawa, Ontario, Canada

Unless otherwise indicated, Scripture references in this book are from the New King James Version.

Edited by Lincoln E. Steed
Designed by Tim Larson
Typeset in 10/12 Century Schoolbook

The author assumes full reponsibility for the accuracy of all facts and quotations cited in this book.

Copyright © 1991 by
Pacific Press Publishing Association
Printed in United States of America
All Rights Reserved

Library of Congress Catalog Number: 90-62307

ISBN 0-8163-1021-1

Contents

Chapter	1	A Dream Come True	7
Chapter	2	Holy Devil of the Czar	18
Chapter	3	Gates of Hell	29
Chapter	4	The Fall of the Wall	40
Chapter	5	Comrades in Christ	49
Chapter	6	Secret of Fatima	60
Chapter	7	Defeat of Barbarossa	70

Chapter 1
A Dream Come True

For many years I've longed to visit the Soviet Union to bring you a firsthand report on fellow Christians there. Thank God, that time has finally come. In the next seven chapters we'll take an unforgettable tour of this remarkable land.

Would you stand with me on Red Square in the heart of Moscow.

Behind us is St. Basil's Cathedral, one of the many churches within the Kremlin complex. There are fourteen of them—fourteen churches right at the headquarters of the Soviet Union. Of course, all of them became museums under Communist rule. Yet despite the prevailing atheism of the last seventy years, these magnificent cathedrals have borne a testimony—a silent, yet powerful testimony to the religious heritage of the Russian people.

Now there is a new yearning for the ancient faith. And surprisingly, religion is respectable again—thanks to the policies of *perestroika* (the restructuring of society under President Mikhail Gorbachev). Across the Soviet Union, there is a tremendous revival of spirituality among Christians, Muslims, and Jewish people. In these pages, as we get to know our Soviet brothers and sisters, I'm sure we'll find much inspiration for our own faith.

You understand that I'm a United States citizen, and I praise God for my land of freedom—but I've noticed that Soviet Christians are equally patriotic for their own homeland. Shall we then set aside political differences and cherish what we have in common? Let's focus on the faith in God that binds our hearts together. After all, we are comrades in Christ!

All right. Let's begin by taking a get-acquainted tour around Moscow, the Soviet capital, starting right in Red Square. This square is a vast open space paved with cobblestones, more than a half mile long. Behind us we see St. Basil's Cathedral, with its onion-shaped towers of red, green, and glistening gold. On the opposite end of Red Square is the dignified red-brick State Historical Museum. To the east is the GUM Department Store, largest of its kind in the Soviet Union.

On our left is Lenin's Tomb, an imposing structure of polished granite honoring the founding father of the Soviet Union. Just behind it is that ancient fortress recognized everywhere as the Kremlin, headquarters of the Soviet government.

The Kremlin, we see, is surrounded by a high wall about a mile and a half long. Five watchtowers loom over it, each topped with big red stars that glow at night. Inside the Kremlin complex is the huge congressional palace, along with a number of gold-domed cathedrals and pale yellow palaces. Some of them function as museums, showcasing the wealth of the ancient czars—magnificent robes, crowns and jewels. Other buildings of the Kremlin provide headquarters for the Soviet government.

Twelve streets branch out from the Kremlin into the city of Moscow. Most famous is Gorki Street, a broad, tree-lined boulevard lined by stores, restaurants, and book shops. One of Moscow's proud landmarks is its main subway station, almost rivaling a palace with its beautiful mosaics.

The subway takes us to the Agricultural Fairgrounds, with its spectacular fountain and flower gardens. On another subway stop we find ourselves looking up at Moscow State University, on a hill overlooking the river. Finally we come to that famous Olympic sports complex, Lenin Stadium.

Of course, there are more than tourist attractions in this vast city of nine million. Moscow has mile after mile of factories and crowded apartments. And beyond the city in the green birch woods are the pleasant country homes of government leaders, scientists, and artists.

No doubt about it, Moscow is a remarkable city. Its history is equally impressive, going back more than eight centuries to a wooden stockade built on a river bank. The roots of its religious life take us back even farther. Christianity sprouted in old Russia in the year 988. It's an intriguing story that transports us to the Ukrainian city of Kiev.

At a picturesque spot along the banks of the Dnieper River, Grand Prince Vladimir I was baptized more than a thousand years ago. His conversion to Christianity was a startling development in a violent, hedonistic life. Vladimir had even murdered some of his own relatives. He also killed two Christians who refused to sacrifice to his pagan gods.

Vladimir knew better. He had already encountered the claims of Christ through his godly grandmother, Olga. Her prayers for him seemed wasted until Vladimir surprised everyone and announced his conversion to Christianity.

The grand prince may have had more than piety in mind in becoming a Christian. You see, the emperor Basil II in Constantinople had promised to give Vladimir his royal

10 COMRADES IN CHRIST

sister, Anna, in marriage if he accepted her Christianity. Besides this compelling motivation, Vladimir needed religion to unify the pagan tribes under his leadership. He explored and rejected Islam, Judaism, and Roman Catholicism before choosing Eastern Orthodox Christianity.

No doubt Vladimir was impressed by what his representatives found when they visited Constantinople, headquarters of the Eastern Orthodox Church. Tradition has it that the splendor of the Cathedral of Hagia Sophia, with its 10,000 flickering candles and gold mosaics, staggered Vladimir's men. They reported: "We knew not whether we were in heaven or on earth, for on earth there is no such splendor or such beauty."

And so Vladimir proclaimed himself a Christian. After his baptism he immediately moved to establish Greek Orthodox Christianity as the official state religion in the lands under his realm. He even issued a decree stating: "Whoever fails to come to the bank of the Dnieper River tomorrow [to be baptized] will be my enemy, be he rich or poor, beggar or slave."

The next day multitudes came here and watched the grand prince arrive with a procession of priests. As the priests chanted the liturgy, Vladimir ordered his people to wade into the water and get baptized. It was a milestone in the history of Russia.

At first thought, this mass baptism might seem to be a wonderful event. The people had been pagans with a yen for human sacrifice; now, by order of their government, they became baptized Christians. Unfortunately, individual conscience didn't seem to matter to Grand Prince Vladimir. He meant well, no doubt, but the Bible teaches that people should be free to choose for themselves about getting baptized. We see this from what Jesus said in Mark 16:16: "He who believes and is baptized will be saved."

A DREAM COME TRUE

We must believe in order to be baptized. This obviously requires the freedom of personal choice. Forcing people to be baptized is no different then making them get married. People have a right to their own choice, don't you think?

The history of Christianity—in Russia as well as in Rome—reveals the sad results of enforcing faith. Whenever the church influences the government to make religious legislation, freedom suffers. The union of church and state in old Russia ultimately helped topple the Czars, paving the way for atheistic Communism to outlaw religious influence. Some of the same factors were at work in the atheistic French Revolution of the eighteenth century.

In the United States we take pride in our religious freedom, and I thank God for it. But you know, we too have had serious problems with religious oppression back in our colonial days. Few of us realize how our spiritual roots are riddled with intolerance.

Several hundred years ago in the American colonies, unbelief was a crime. Faith was enforced by law. Believe it or not, certain religious offenses were even punishable by death. That was before the American Constitution with the Bill of Rights guaranteed religious liberty. But Bible prophecy predicts that the future will bring a reversion to religious repression. We'll see this in a later chapter.

Church history shows us, again and again, that government must not interfere with religious matters. Certainly civil morality must be enforced by law and order—or else murderers, robbers, and rapists will ravage society. But when it comes to personal religious expression, the conscience cannot be compelled. Every individual must be free to love God—or to withhold love from Him—without interference from government.

Notice what Jesus taught here in Matthew 22:21: "Render therefore to Caesar the things that are Caesar's,

12 COMRADES IN CHRIST

and to God the things that are God's."

So things that belong to Caesar—civil government—and things that belong to God—religious matters—must remain separate, lest we return to the days of religious persecution.

Now let's go back to Grand Prince Vladimir in Russia. Under his forceful leadership the Slavic tribes united into a political power headquartered in Kiev. Meanwhile, 700 miles to the south in Constantinople, trouble was brewing with Rome.

The religious rivalry between Constantinople and Rome had its roots in events of the fourth century. Way back then, several hundred years after Christ, the Roman Emperor Constantine converted to Christianity. His experience was quite similar to Vladimir's of Russia. Both had been pagans, enemies of Christianity, who experienced sudden and dramatic conversions. And both leaders forced religion on their subjects. Constantine marched his soldiers into the sea to be baptized.

Then, seeking to Christianize the Roman Empire, in the year 321 he declared Sunday the national day of rest. The seventh-day Sabbath of the Bible had already fallen into neglect in many areas, but Constantine made it official. Eventually a compromised form of Christianity became the official state religion. Not long thereafter, the Church of Rome began persecuting all who resisted her teachings.

How did the church become powerful enough to persecute? It filled a vacuum of leadership created when Constantine moved his capital from Rome. Seeking to escape economic problems and the threat of invasion by barbarian tribes, the emperor relocated 800 miles east, establishing Constantinople as his capital (now Istanbul, Turkey). From that time onward, the western part of the empire was dominated by the bishop of Rome.

Eventually, the city of Rome did fall to the barbarian

A DREAM COME TRUE 13

tribes. The church, however, managed to Christianize the invaders, thus maintaining its control of the western empire. To the east, Constantinople remained secure for a couple of centuries.

Then came fierce raids by Muslim armies. One of their massive naval assaults is said to have involved 1,800 ships. The Christian defenders counterattacked with a terrifying secret weapon known as Greek fire, which burned more ferociously in water than on land. The exact formula of Greek fire remains a secret to this day. It wrought terrible havoc among the Muslim attackers. Their forces were defeated—Constantinople remained in Christian hands for the next 700 years.

The church in Constantinople had no secret weapon for its spiritual war with fellow Christians in Rome. The dispute between the Eastern Orthodox and Roman Catholic churches centered around the pontiff's claim of supreme authority over all Christians. They argued over other matters—among them the seventh-day Sabbath.

Rome was determined to eradicate Sabbath keeping throughout Christendom. You see, centuries after Sunday became the law of the empire, little pockets of believers still worshiped on the Bible Sabbath. We have record of Sabbath keeping in areas as diverse as Egypt, France, Turkey, Palestine, Syria, Italy, France, and Yugoslavia. Evidence indicates that in Ireland, Saint Patrick kept the Sabbath. (You may find that surprising, as I did.) In many of these places both Sabbath and Sunday were honored.

The Eastern Orthodox leaders had no problem worshiping on Sunday, but they protested Rome's insistence upon making the Sabbath a day of gloom and fasting. They said such abuse of the Sabbath had no foundation in Scripture and seriously altered the intended character of the Sabbath as a day of joy.

14 COMRADES IN CHRIST

Pope Leo IX refused the reforms demanded by Patriarch Caerularius of Constantinople. Tempers flared. The pontiff dispatched his representative with an official document denouncing Eastern Orthodox Christians as living on a level with the devil. The patriarch did not appreciate Rome's assessment of his character. Not surprisingly, the pope and the patriarch excommunicated each other and their followers, resulting in what we know as the Great Schism.

This separation between Rome and Constantinople began in the year 1054. For the next nine centuries the Roman Catholics and Greek Orthodox shunned each other. In recent times they have resumed dialogue, but their basic incompatibility remains—Rome's determination that the pontiff be recognized as supreme authority over Christians everywhere.

You may find yourself wondering, What does the dispute between Constantinople and Rome have to do with religion in the Soviet Union? Quite a bit. We've been hearing on the news how the Russian Orthodox Church finds itself at odds with Roman Catholics. The roots of this misunderstanding can be traced to that Great Schism of 1054. Grand Prince Vladimir, you recall, had aligned himself with Rome's rival, Eastern Orthodox Christianity.

How, then, did the Russian church wean itself from the influence of Constantinople? To begin with, Vladimir wanted to nationalize the church of Russia, making it the powerful preserver of national identity. His son, who succeeded him, Yaroslav the Wise, took his father's efforts even further. Yaroslav determined to make Kiev the rival of Constantinople.

That never happened. The invasion of Mongols from the east forced the Russians to move their capital to Moscow. But through the unifying influence of national Christianity, Russia emerged intact from the 240-year domina-

A DREAM COME TRUE   15

tion of the Mongols. This reign of terror finally ended in 1480, during the rule of Czar Ivan the Great. The invaders were camped across the river from Moscow, when unexpectedly, they withdrew. Mongol rule was over. Ivan the Great had succeeded in preserving Russia.

Meanwhile, the city of Constantinople finally fell into Muslim hands. The invaders' huge guns hurled such heavy stones that the city's thick walls crumbled in 1453. That was the downfall of Eastern Orthodox Christianity. Ivan the Great determined to fill the void by proclaiming Moscow to be the third Rome, the new center of Christianity in place of old Rome and Constantinople.

The czar moved quickly to establish his empire of church and state. In harmony with his ambitions for a third Rome, Ivan hired Italian architects to renovate the magnificent Assumption Cathedral. And to safeguard the Kremlin against future assaults, he built a brick wall around his fortress as thick as twenty feet, with fortified towers at the corners and towers in between. According to legend, the design included a number of secret tunnels extending beyond the Kremlin walls.

Ivan the Great's massive building project occupied thirty years. Much of his Italian Kremlin still stands after five centuries. Most spectacular, perhaps, is the Palace of Facets. Its main chamber, the most celebrated room in the Kremlin, served both as throne room and reception hall for Ivan and his successors. When President Gorbachev welcomed American President Reagan to the palace chamber in 1988, he maintained a tradition dating back to Czar Ivan the Great.

After Ivan passed from the scene, the power of the Russian Orthodox Church grew to equal and even exceed the authority of civil rulers. The czars were regarded as God's servants under the guidance of the church.

That lasted until 1721, when Czar Peter the Great decreed that the church had become too powerful. He delegated to a political appointee the operation of religion, making it a subservient arm of the state. Nevertheless, until the twentieth century, the Russian Orthodox Church still possessed the power to persecute non-Orthodox Christians.

What about religious liberty in the Soviet Union today? In one of these chapters we will discuss that vital question with a representative of the Soviet government. I think you'll be delighted with what you'll read from him.

Thank God, things really are changing in the Soviet Union. We see it on the news, we read it in the papers. Recently the *Los Angeles Times* headlined a story, "Bible is a Real Page-turner at Soviet Fair." It described the thrilling scene at the Moscow International Book Fair.

Word spread that a Christian publisher was distributing Bibles at its booth. Soon eager crowds had snatched up the supply of 10,000 New Testaments. And more people kept coming.

Now, it so happened that the American Atheist Association had a booth nearby, featuring none other than Madelyn Murray O'Hair. Evidently Mrs. O'Hair and her friends thought they would find a welcome among the Soviet people for their godless publications. One was entitled, "Trash the Bible"—but few seemed interested in trashing the Bible. They would rather treasure their own copy of God's Word.

So there they were, forming long lines that stretched around the corner in front of the American Atheist booth. Madelyn Murray O'Hair reportedly became furious. Not only were these citizens of a supposedly atheistic state ignoring her godless propaganda—they were jamming the aisles, blocking her booth in their scramble to get God's Word.

A DREAM COME TRUE

Near-chaos reigned. The horrified Mrs. O'Hair summoned authorities and demanded that they control the Bible-hungry crowd. Someone climbed onto a table shouting, "Please stand back!"

But, no. The people of Russia would not be denied their precious Bibles. They had waited long enough, and now their time had come.

With the supply of Bibles gone, 17,000 extra requests came in for Bibles to be sent. Many pleaded in halting English, "Will you really send my Bible?"

Praise God, it's a new day in the Soviet Union, as Madelyn Murray O'Hair discovered. An incredible experience! I find myself not only thrilled, but challenged—how about you? Are we as determined as those Soviet citizens to cherish God's Word? Are we as willing to study its message and walk in the light?

God help us catch on to their commitment!

Chapter 2
Holy Devil of the Czar

The holy devil, they called him—Rasputin, one of history's most riveting yet revolting characters. He was the peasant priest who wielded fatal control over Czar Nicholas and the empress of Russia. What was the secret of his mysterious power?

Come with me to the old winter palace of the czars in Leningrad.

Before the revolution of 1917, Leningrad, known as St. Petersburg, was the capital of the Russian Empire. It became the stomping ground of Rasputin.

Rasputin—his very name has intrigued the world for the seven decades since his death. The long-haired, wild-eyed peasant from Siberia has been memorialized in more than twenty movies—besides dozens of documentaries, miniseries, and plays.

Rasputin's rough-hewn appearance belied his role as favored guest of the royal court. He gloried in the contrast between his peasant mannerisms and the polished etiquette of the czar's social circle. As he mingled with guests entering the palace with their fashionable furs, Rasputin thrust his coarse black tunic into the arms of the startled footman. Then, striding confidently into the crowded ballroom, the hulking thirty-three-year-old became the immediate center of attention.

He grabbed the hands of noblemen and their wives with his own huge hands, gazing fiercely into their eyes. He interrogated them about personal matters, offering intimate advice. Flaunting his lack of education, he unabashedly belched forth crude language. He even plunged his unwashed hands into his favorite fish soup.

Incredible as it may seem, the uncouth peasant from Siberia charmed the hearts of St. Petersburg's social elite. His barbarian manners attracted rather than repelled his titled admirers. To them, he was an exotic diversion in a restless, meaningless society.

One woman recalled her first encounter with Rasputin, as recorded in the classic biography *Nicholas and Alexandra*. "Our eyes met," she said, "his eyes held mine, those shining steel-like eyes which seemed to read one's inmost thoughts. He came forward and took my hand. . . . 'Thou are worried. . . . Well, nothing in life is worth worrying over. . . . It is necessary to have faith. God alone is thy help.'"

Rasputin embellished his conversations with ancient Russian proverbs and quotes from the Bible. He became a sought-out spiritual counselor, regarded as a holy man of God.

In reality, Rasputin was anything but devout. As a carousing young man, he had earned the nickname by which he was known the rest of his life. You see, in the Russian language, *Rasputin* means "licentious, dissolute." He did profess a dramatic conversion to Christianity. Returning from a pilgrimage to the Holy Land, he affirmed a fervent faith in Christ. Actually, he never abandoned the wild orgies and drunkenness for which he became a legend. How then did he manage to win the confidence of church leaders?

They saw an undeniable spiritual power emanating from his blazing, hypnotic eyes. And so the religious hierarchy of Russia endorsed Rasputin as God's servant to the royal family.

The peasant priest seemed to have the power of divine healing—and the royal family desperately needed healing when the czar's son became ill. The boy suffered from an internal hemorrhage so serious that funeral arrangements were made. In that crisis hour a telegram arrived from Rasputin with the startling message: "The little one will not die." Immediately the bleeding stopped. Rasputin's prophecy came true.

The aunt of Czar Nicholas testified, "There is no doubt about [Rasputin's healing powers]. I saw those miraculous effects with my own eyes, and that more than once. I also know that the most prominent doctors of the day had to admit it."

Empress Alexandra and Czar Nicholas became convinced beyond question that Rasputin must be God's messenger—how else could he work such miracles? they wondered. Before long the wild peasant through his healing power virtually controlled the royal family. The fall of the Russian Empire was not long in following.

One historian concluded, "The fatal influence of that man [Rasputin] was the principal cause of death of those who thought to find in him their salvation."

Now, let's take a break from the adventures of Rasputin and come back to the 1990s. This matter of faith healing is quite relevant to our day, you know. Faith healers crisscross the country in the name of God. Many of them are charlatans, no doubt, deceiving their audiences with pretended miracles. But is it possible that some of them have real miracle-working power? And if so, is that gift of healing necessarily from God?

Many Christians automatically assume that any supernatural power must come from God. But the case of Rasputin raises the troubling question, Can Satan actually heal? And if so, how can we tell the working of the devil from the working of God?

Important questions, wouldn't you say? Absolutely vital to understand. Let's open our Bibles and learn the truth about miracles. We turn first to the book of Revelation to learn about deceivers of the last days: "They are the spirits of devils, working miracles, which go forth unto the kings of the earth and of the whole world, to gather them to the battle of that great day of God Almighty" (Revelation 16:14, KJV).

There it is—just before the coming of Christ, demons will work miracles. Genuine miracles from the devil! And believe it or not, these satanic powers perform their wonders in the name of Jesus Christ. Our Lord Himself warned:

> "Many will say to me on that day, 'Lord, Lord, did we not prophesy in your name, and in your name drive out demons and perform many miracles?' Then I will tell them plainly, 'I never knew you. Away from me, you evildoers!' " (Matthew 7:22-23, NIV).

So false prophets like Rasputin will use Christ's name to practice evil and lawlessness. Through these deceivers the devil performs all kinds of lying wonders to entrap the unsuspecting. Evidently miracles themselves are not proof of God's presence.

Never forget it, friend. Some miracles are the work of the enemy done in the spirit of lawlessness—violating God's law. Listen to this crystal-clear distinction between genuine Christianity and the enemy's counterfeit: "This is the love of God, that we keep His commandments. And His commandments are not burdensome" (1 John 5:3).

Genuine love for God is the test, and true love for God obeys His commandments. So love for God means more than a warm feeling in our hearts when we worship. The proof of Christian love is not miracles, not speaking in tongues. The proof is keeping God's commandments.

Rasputin, despite his pretended claim to holiness, trampled upon the Ten Commandments. Ladies of the czar's court fell prey to his adulterous advances. The supposed holy man urged the women to go ahead and sin with him. He assured them that only after they indulged in sin could they appreciate the blessing of forgiveness. Countless women succumbed to Rasputin's seduction—after all, he had miraculous power. So he must be from God, they reasoned.

They should have known better. Rasputin's contempt for the Ten Commandments betrayed his satanic sponsorship.

In recent years in North America, we've also been shocked and saddened by spiritual leaders claiming to have the power of God while indulging themselves in lawless behavior. We've seen how the devil abuses the gifts of the Holy Spirit in the name of Jesus. He counterfeits the gift of healing; he counterfeits the gift of tongues.

Does it surprise you that the devil can speak in tongues? After all, he is an angel fallen, so he can speak any language of earth or heaven.

Please let me warn you with all my heart—beware. Beware of false tongues, false miracles, false healings.

At this point you may be wondering, Why would Satan, who loves to hurt people, want to bring us healing? He wants control of our lives, that's why. Just as he used Rasputin to deceive the people of Russia and plunge them into perdition.

HOLY DEVIL OF THE CZAR 23

Rasputin forged his stranglehold upon the empire by winning the blessing of church leaders. Father John of Kronstadt and the saintly Bishop Theophan, two of the most revered priests in Russia, endorsed Rasputin's ministry. They were deceived by his apparently fervent "faith," and his ability to work such miracles.

As time went on, however, the priests had second thoughts. They heard the embarrassed confessions of women led into sin by Rasputin. The priests, being men of integrity, were horrified. Convinced at last that Rasputin's debauchery disqualified him from being a man of God—despite whatever miracles he could perform—they urged the empress to banish the imposter.

But the damage was done by the priests' previous endorsement of Rasputin. Instead of exiling his carousing "holy man," Czar Nicholas dismissed Father John. Rasputin boasted, "I have shut his trap."

Listen—if godly spiritual leaders can be fooled by satanic miracles, don't you think all of us ought to beware? We have the warning of God's Word that the devil will perform his final deceptions through miracles. So let's watch out for counterfeit agents of the Holy Spirit. Keep your eyes open and your Bible close by!

Now let me say this—there is such a thing as divine healing.

Praise God, I've seen many cases in which the genuine healing power of God rescued sick ones from the brink of death. But I've also seen many true believers die, despite their magnificent faith. And you have too, haven't you?

Why does God let it happen?

The fact is that there are many things we never understand in this old world. God's ways of working go beyond human comprehension.

Even the apostle Paul found himself perplexed. He

couldn't get himself healed of his mysterious affliction called a "thorn in the flesh." Three times he begged God for deliverance. Finally he accepted this suffering and went on with life. Actually, this illness proved to be a blessing, keeping him humble and dependent upon God.

Keep in mind that apostle Paul's lack of healing didn't mean he lacked faith. You recall Paul even had faith to raise a man from death, something faith healers today seem unable to do. Think about that. Faith healers now claim to have all the Pentecostal power of New Testament times, yet we don't see them interrupting funerals to raise the dead to life, do we? Why not? Could it be that this matter of faith and healing isn't as cut and dried as they say it is?

Well-meaning Christians insist God will definitely heal all sickness when we have faith. That sounds wonderful at first. But their guarantee of instant healing may not turn out to be such good news after all—it can create a tremendous load of guilt.

Let me explain. If faith ought to always bring healing, then those who remain ill must not have faith. The sick are somehow not "spiritual enough" to be healed.

This type of thinking gets more serious. Listen: If the faith that saves me ought to heal me, then when I'm not healed, maybe I'm not saved. Can you see the potential for a problem here?

Many dying saints cry to God to be healed, yet they remain sick. So they begin to doubt their salvation. They carry a false burden of guilt even worse than their pain.

Thank God, salvation does not depend upon whether or not we get a particular answer to prayer. Instead, being saved depends upon whether we trust Jesus, exchanging what the world offers for what He offers.

It's absolutely vital to understand this matter of miraculous healing. Otherwise we find ourselves confused by all kinds of questions. For example, sometimes I'm asked, Is it a lack of faith to take medication? Well, some enthusiastic Christians imagine so. Others point out that the same God who designed our bodies has given physicians wisdom to prescribe care for it.

One more point about faith and healing. God expects us to care for our bodies, which are the temple of His Holy Spirit. How do you think He feels when Christians ignore the warning of medical science about clogging their arteries with cholesterol? They indulge in all the greasy steaks they might crave, and then they think they can say a magic prayer demanding instant healing from heart disease! And they call this exercising faith! Perhaps a better term for it might be presumption—prayer abuse.

Now, having shared all this caution and counsel, let me say again—I believe in divine healing by faith. All I'm saying is that God expects us to cooperate with His principles of good health. And when we do become ill anyway, true faith trusts God to heal us in His own time and way, as He knows best.

Sometimes He does heal immediately. Sometimes gradually. And sometimes He waits to heal us until the resurrection when Jesus comes.

Let me ask you, Does it take more faith to demand to be healed now or to commit your body to God and let Him bring healing when He knows is best? Tell me, which takes more faith—to get what I want now or to let God work in His time and way?

And remember the Bible warning that the devil will work miracles in the name of Jesus. So let's reject everything that operates out of harmony with God's commandments. Only then can we be secure from the final deceptions. I leave you with this final word of counsel from God's Word:

26 COMRADES IN CHRIST

"There is a way that seems right to a man, but its end is the way of death" (Proverbs 16:25, NKJV).

Rasputin's evil ways brought about his untimely death at the age of forty-four. He was drowned the night of December 30, 1916.

The fateful rendezvous took place after five Russian nobles, distressed about Rasputin's stranglehold on the empire, met to plot his death. They determined to poison him in the cellar of the Moika Palace. The bait for their trap was the promise of a party with Princess Irina, famous for her beauty, someone Rasputin longed to spend time with.

On the night of death the assassins welcomed Rasputin at the palace. With the tune of "Yankee Doodle Dandy" playing happily upstairs, Rasputin ate several poisoned cakes, washing them down with poisoned wine. Although the food had enough potassium cyanide to kill an ox or two, the amazing priest didn't drop dead. He just seemed a bit dazed.

The assassins wondered what to do about their uncooperative victim. For the next two hours or so, they entertained him with music. Finally they lost patience with their poison and shot him through the heart.

A physician on the scene pronounced Rasputin dead. But then, horror of horrors, his eyes fluttered open, and the hulking maniac roared to life. Furious, he lunged at his would-be killers, chasing them out into the snow-covered courtyard.

There the incredible hulk was shot again and again. Finally the assassins tied him up in a blue curtain and dragged him to the banks of the Neva River. Rasputin was thrown into the icy river, where he finally drowned.

Not long after Rasputin's death came the fall of the empire he led into perdition. Later, Czar Nicholas and his family were arrested. The night of July 16, 1918, the royal household met their bloody fate. It was their reward for following the evil priest—a tragic forecast of what will happen to all who pursue spiritual deception.

Now I'd like to leave you with a word of hope. The story itself will be sad, but it reveals by contrast the glorious heritage God offers us in Christ.

Out of the ruins of the fallen Russian Empire emerged the legend of Anastasia, daughter of the czar. It's never been documented beyond question, but many historians are convinced that Anastasia survived the assassination of her family. On the night of death a daring soldier rescued the beautiful young duchess, smuggling her out of the country on a farm cart to Romania. There they were married.

Then followed a chain of tragic events for Anastasia. Her new husband was killed on the streets of Bucharest. The young widow escaped to Berlin to seek out her mother's relatives. She had been there less than a week when she fell into a canal.

Rescued again from death, she refused to divulge her identity for fear of sharing her family's fate. Frustrated authorities committed the homeless young wanderer to a public mental hospital. Finally, after repeated questioning, she confessed the truth—she was Grand Duchess Anastasia, daughter of the late czar.

Now that her royal identity was known, Anastasia began a long battle to win the rights to her family's wealth, stashed in the Bank of England. Amid conflicting testimony she never succeeded in documenting her pedigree. Anastasia finally declared in frustration, "I know perfectly well who I am. I don't need to prove it to myself."

How different from Anastasia's frustration is the security God offers us in Christ. Anastasia was rescued from death only to become a wandering widow, but our

Lord saves us from death to the triumph of life eternal. Anastasia never managed to prove her royal identity to the satisfaction of the judge. But for us, the heavenly Judge Himself claims us as His royal children—we may rest secure in His acceptance. Anastasia never won access to her family's wealth, but we have continual and complete access by faith to heaven's eternal storehouse.

Thank God for what He offers us in Christ! I ask you— Are you a child of the King, or are you a prodigal wandering far from the Father's house? Have you yielded your life to the Lord, putting your trust in the Lord Jesus Christ?

Chapter 3
Gates of Hell

Mikhail Gorbachev . . . Winston Churchill . . . Franklin Roosevelt . . . Adolph Hitler. The twentieth century has seen more than its share of world-shaking leaders.

Pope John Paul II . . . Ronald Reagan . . . Mao Tse-tung. Perhaps the leader who shaped our century the most is Vladimir Ulyanov, known to the world as Lenin.

Nothing in the background of Vladimir Lenin would have predicted his incredible influence upon our century. He burst upon the scene in an hour of opportunity, when Russian society was struggling to recover from the abusive reign of the czars.

For three centuries, ever since Peter the Great, the czarist house of Romanov had ruled with an iron fist. Life back then was bleak for the peasants, a mere passing of seasons between birth and death. By the mid-1800s, wealthy landowners oppressed peasants in what amounted to slavery. Although emancipation came in 1861, fertile land available for farming was scarce.

In some ways the peasants found themselves worse off after liberation than they had been as slaves. Many fled to the cities, encouraged by the czar's regime to find work in factories. But there they only exchanged one form of bondage for another. Inhumane working conditions and incredibly low wages cursed their lives more than ever.

Such was the lot of the peasants and working class at the turn of this century. They weren't the only ones yearning for change from the czar's rigid rule. The rising business and professional class also desired a democratic government unhindered by the whims of the czar. While the people of the palace pursued their endless pleasures, a new word crept into the Russian vocabulary—*revolution.*

Discontent boiled over in St. Petersburg, now Leningrad. Tragedy struck during the arctic-cold winter of 1905 when the working class exercised the only weapons always available—demonstrations and strikes. Their demands for bread and breathing room were modest, but Czar Nicholas branded them as enemies of the state. He summoned into action his mounted police to brutally suppress the demonstrations.

The crisis climaxed on January 22, known ever since as "Bloody Sunday." On that fateful day the czar's dreaded Cossacks fired on a crowd of peaceful demonstrators. A thousand fell dead; 5,000 were wounded. Hundreds of women and children spilled their blood.

The massacre of Bloody Sunday only deepened the determination of the Russian people to overthrow their government. The czar's days were numbered.

Unrest erupted again in 1912, only to be quickly quelled by bullets. Exile and execution became commonplace. Among those already put to death for conspiracy against the czar was Lenin's own brother, Alexander. The future leader of Russia quietly determined to avenge his family's loss.

Studying law by day, Lenin devoted his nights to propagating the socialist principles of Karl Marx. But the czar's secret police, alerted to his underground activities, imprisoned Lenin without trial and exiled him to Siberia.

There he married a fellow revolutionary, and together they secretly printed and circulated antigovernment Marxist publications.

Meanwhile, at the czar's palace, life went on as usual. The royal family and their elite circle of socialites let the good times roll, ignoring the volcano of unrest simmering around them. "Don't worry, be happy!" seemed to be the motto at the palace. Parties and picnics were more pleasant to contemplate than the fall of the house of Romanov.

Czar Nicholas and Empress Alexandra were indulgent parents, treating their children much better than their subjects. It was this devotion to their gravely ill son that entangled them with Rasputin.

The perverted faith healer strengthened his stranglehold over Russia during World War I. He took advantage of the situation when Czar Nicholas traveled away from the palace to encourage his people in repelling the German invaders. Russians everywhere responded to their czar's patriotic appeals, forgetting for the time his oppression. But when the Russian army suffered horrible casualties, national morale plummeted—especially when mass starvation threatened the cities.

Once again, civil unrest erupted in Russia, this time in the midst of world war. When food shortages sparked street demonstrations, garrison soldiers refused to suppress the famished masses. The czar, without support from the military, was unable to enslave his subjects any longer. Officials demanded that he transfer power to a parliamentary government. Finally, in March of 1917, the evil empire came to an end as Czar Nicholas resigned. The 300-year-old Romanov dynasty was history.

The fate of government was now in the hands of the people. As the provisional government struggled for survival, Lenin emerged from exile with the rallying cry

"Peace, land, and bread!" He declared a worker's revolution against the new leadership.

Lenin's soldiers prepared for civil war. The night of October 25, 1917, the Bolshevik Revolution began. At 9:25 a shot fired on the cruiser *Aurora* launched the attack upon the czar's winter palace. Within a few days Lenin and his Red Army had won. The Soviet Union became a Communist empire.

It should not surprise us that the new Soviet government was hostile toward religion. After all, the Russian church had aligned itself with the czar's evil empire. How very sad.

Long ago in ancient times, religion had served to unify Russia and promote the national good. But somehow during the centuries it became the tool of oppression. In the final years of the czars, with the wicked priest Rasputin manipulating both church and state, organized religion dug its own grave. Many Russians rejoiced when Communism resolved to bury the established church bureaucracy.

So it was that one of the first legal acts of the Soviet government following the revolution was to strip the church of its political power. Despite this, personal freedom of conscience was supposed to be protected. The new constitution, which separated church from state, defended the right of Soviet citizens to profess any religion or none at all. Tragically, though, many of the freedoms guaranteed under the constitution were quickly lost to believers.

In the 1920s, the Soviet government closed churches and made them into museums. Priests and pastors who resisted became prisoners, and church members were converted into Communist party members instead. Lenin's war against religion intensified under his successor, Joseph Stalin. In 1929 Stalin amended the Soviet constitution to stamp out religious freedom. By the end of

1938, more than 70,000 churches had been closed, along with all monasteries and seminaries. Thousands, perhaps millions, were massacred for their faith.

Of course, it wasn't just the church that suffered under Stalin—the whole system of legal justice was corrupt. Farmers, military officers, and even loyal Communists were shot, starved, or killed slowly in Siberian exile. It was the church, however, that was Stalin's special object of attack. Believing that religion was not just "the opium of the people," but poison as well, he unleashed the full horror of his persecution upon believers.

God only knows how much the Soviet faithful suffered under Stalin. "That could never happen in America," many of us may be thinking. Actually, Bible prophecy foretells that religious oppression will indeed rear its ugly head in our land of freedom. Ultimately a death decree will result for those whose faith in Christ leads them to keep all of God's commandments. We'll see this in a later chapter.

Religious persecution in America would undermine our legal system with its protection for the accused. The way it stands now, if judges are prejudiced against defendants, our law demands they be disqualified. Yet the ancient legal code of the Hebrews went even further in protecting the rights of the accused.

You see, in Old Testament times, the defense of the accused was a duty so sacred, the judge refused to delegate that job to an attorney. He himself served as the defender of the accused. The *Jewish Encyclopedia* explains that "attorneys at law are unknown in Jewish law." Their legal code required judges to "lean always to the side of the defendant and give him the advantage of every possible doubt."

Witnesses of the crime pressed charges, while the judge promoted the case of the defendant, biased in favor of acquittal. Only when overwhelmed by the evidence would the judge abandon his defense of the accused and reluctantly pronounce condemnation.

Interesting system, wouldn't you say?

Lessons from the Hebrew law court abound for us today. Many Christians fear to face God as their Judge. If they only understood the biblical method of judgment, they would realize that He is on our side! He takes upon Himself the job of our defense!

Well, now, if God is defending us in the heavenly judgment, who is accusing us? You guessed it—the devil. The Bible calls him the "accuser of our brethren," who "accuses them before God day and night . . ." (Revelation 12:10).

Apparently Satan is jealous about our going to heaven, where he used to live when he was Lucifer, prince of the angels. And so he accuses God's children of being unfit to pass through the pearly gates.

But we are unworthy! So how can we escape the accusations of the enemy? Notice: "They overcame him by the blood of the Lamb" (Revelation 12:11).

It's through the blood of Jesus—and by His blood alone—that you and I can overcome the devil's accusations. God cannot deny Satan's contention that we are imperfect, falling far short of His ideal. But in the blood shed on Calvary's cross our Judge finds the evidence He needs to defend us and pronounce us innocent. So in the name of Christ, God dismisses Satan's charges. He endorses the assurance of salvation we have enjoyed in Jesus since we accepted Him.

Thrilling, wouldn't you say? Such an understanding of God's judgment makes us feel confident about our salvation in Christ!

My friend, if you haven't yet entrusted your life to Jesus, if you haven't yet put your faith in His saving blood, I urge you to do so today.

Now back to the history of Christianity in the Soviet Union. We talked about how, in old Russia under the czars, the church abused the political system. Then, with Communism, the pendulum swung to the other extreme, and the political system abused the church.

A truce of sorts came during the 1940s. World War II, which brought such turmoil to the world, brought some relief to Russia's persecuted church. You see, Stalin needed the support of church leaders to rally the nation for the war against the Nazis, so he relaxed his repression against religion.

The Russian Orthodox Church suddenly took on new life. The number of parishes skyrocketed from about 1,500 to 20,000, and eight seminaries were reopened, along with some monasteries. After the war, the church hierarchy sought to continue its policy of cooperation with the government, even serving as a political mouthpiece. Nevertheless, persecution of believers resumed with fury.

Yet through it all, God's people survived. And why not? The Lord had promised to preserve His church. Speaking of Himself to His disciples, Jesus declared: "Upon this rock I will build my church; and the gates of hell shall not prevail against it" (Matthew 16:18, KJV).

Thank God, nothing could ever destroy Christ's precious church—though many through the ages have tried. First the religious establishment in Christ's own day persecuted the early disciples. Then the pagan Roman government. After that, the church itself, fallen from grace, persecuted its own members who refused to compromise their faith. Here in the twentieth century, governments have waged war against God's people. Lenin and Stalin believed religion would disappear when the older generation of churchgoers died. That didn't happen, just as Christ had promised.

How many Christians are there in the Soviet Union

now? Estimates place Russian Orthodox believers at fifty to sixty million. There are 4.5 million Roman Catholics and 3.5 million Ukrainian Catholics. The three million Protestants include Baptists, Pentecostals, and Seventh-day Adventists. In addition to the Christian family of believers, the Soviet Union is home to at least forty million Muslims and many Jewish people—even Buddhists.

Apparently the people of the Soviet Union are unchangeably religious. And let me tell you, their faith in God has not diminished their patriotism. Stalin tried to force an unnatural choice on the people—religion or patriotism. Soviet leaders now understand that believers can indeed be good citizens.

And why not? The stated goal of Soviet society is social justice for all its people. Christians believe in social justice too. Why shouldn't the church survive and thrive in Soviet society?

President Mikhail Gorbachev acknowledged the vital role of believers in the Soviet Union during his historic visit with the pope. He eloquently expressed his conviction that religious values offer great benefit to the nation. Faith in God provides a weapon in the war against alcoholism, drug abuse, prostitution, corruption, and general moral deterioration.

Soviet leaders now regard believers as essential to the moral fabric of their nation. Christians are no longer their enemy. Hundreds of religious prisoners have been released, churches and monasteries have reopened, and Christian leaders frequently air their views on Soviet television. Millions of Bibles freely circulate throughout the nation.

My own Seventh-day Adventist Church is opening a new publishing house not far from Moscow. Through nothing less than a miracle, equipment from Scandinavia became available—a printing press for Bibles, complete with plates already prepared in the Russian language. Many thousands of Bibles and other religious books will be pouring forth from the press to quench the spiritual thirst of the Soviet people.

How times have changed! How much has been accomplished! And we thank God with all our hearts for the new legislation guaranteeing religious freedom. It's now permissible to provide religious education for children—a striking development. Churches now enjoy full legal status. Christians are free to share the gospel of Jesus Christ without restriction.

One area of vital interest to me is religious radio and television. One of our Soviet broadcasters is the dynamic young pastor Peter Kulakov. I'm thrilled to see the beginnings of gospel proclamation over the Soviet airwaves. Let me say it again—thank God for what's happening in the Soviet Union!

Soviet believers recently celebrated the 1,000-year anniversary of Christianity in their nation. After decades of silence, church bells rang joyfully.

We can only wonder what the future may hold. One thing is certain—President Gorbachev treasures the support of Soviet believers as a fundamental ingredient of his ambitious reconstruction. We have assured him of our prayers.

And now our chapter must come to a close. But first let me share the thrilling story of Boris Kornfeld. He was a Jewish medical doctor accused by Stalin for some political offense and imprisoned at a former concentration camp outside Ekibastuz. As Charles Colson mentions in his outstanding book, *Loving God*, Dr. Kornfeld became a Christian while in prison. Quietly he began witnessing for Christ.

One day he treated a young man suffering from intestinal cancer—and an obvious spiritual malaise even more serious. The patient, shaking with fever, missed much of the good doctor's testimony of faith. But he understood enough that afternoon and evening to be impressed with the possibility of freedom in the Lord Jesus Christ.

Late that night, with the guardhouse lights glaring outside, Dr. Kornfeld summed up his confession with the whispered words: "On the whole, you know, I have become convinced that there is no punishment that comes to us in this life on earth which is undeserved."

The patient realized he was hearing an amazing admission. This man was a persecuted Jew who once considered himself innocent. Now he proclaimed that everyone deserves to suffer—but thank God, Jesus Christ took our place on Calvary's cross. Jesus suffered in our place. By accepting His sacrifice, we can stand clean before God, bound for eternal life in heaven.

The young patient drifted off to sleep that night with Dr. Kornfeld's testimony resounding in his heart. Early next morning he woke to the sound of commotion. During the night, someone had attacked Dr. Kornfeld as he slept and murdered him with a hammer.

As the doctor's lifeless body was carried out, his patient opened his heart to new life in Jesus Christ. "God of the universe," he cried, "I believe You!" And the gates of heaven opened wide to that repenting sinner, imprisoned there within the gates of hell.

That young man lived to leave the gulag and tell the world his story. He has become one of the most important moral voices of our time—Alexander Solzhenitsyn. The world may never honor the name of the Jewish doctor who witnessed for Christ in that dark gulag, but millions of Christians today thank God for Solzhenitsyn's testimony.

My friend, I don't know what you might be suffering right now.

Maybe you are languishing in a prison cell, feeling forgotten by God and man. Perhaps instead you are imprisoned by pain or in financial bondage. Maybe holy wedlock has become a prison of unhappy deadlock. Or you may find yourself trapped within the gates of hell in bondage to cocaine, alcohol, or tobacco.

Whatever your imprisonment may be, please know that God cares about you. He really loves you—and He has power to forgive you and set you free! You might continue to suffer in the body, but your spirit can rejoice in the freedom only Jesus can give.

Chapter 4
The Fall of the Wall

On August 13, 1961, Berliners stared disbelievingly as workers began building a huge wall—this cold, gray barrier splitting their city east from west. For nearly three decades, its 100-mile stretch of concrete, barbed wire, and armed patrols separated neighbors, friends, and even families. I was there in Berlin on the twenty-fifth anniversary of the Wall and witnessed the unspeakable pain it brought to the people of Germany.

Then suddenly the Wall came down. The watching world could hardly believe their eyes. Thousands of East Germans surged through to freedom as stunned border guards, trained to shoot, could only wave them on. West Berliners with open arms welcomed their unexpected visitors. Strangers locked in warm embrace, mingling their tears. Loved ones long separated found themselves together again.

Together again! Incredible but true—the Berlin Wall was no more. Joyful Germans danced in the streets. And the fall of the Wall was only the beginning. Almost overnight, it seemed, freedom became an irresistible force throughout Eastern Europe. Poland, Czechoslovakia, Hungary, Bulgaria—finally, even Romania. Nobody, not even the most

THE FALL OF THE WALL 41

optimistic observer of world affairs, had expected so much so soon.

The rebirth of Eastern Europe was possible because of what happened at the Kremlin. The Soviet government's policy of *perestroika* gave the green light for East Bloc countries to move ahead with their own restructuring.

The Soviet people themselves have enjoyed unimaginable new freedoms—freedom to own their own land, freedom of unrestricted media, and best of all, freedom of conscience. I witnessed firsthand the new freedom when worshiping with my fellow Seventh-day Adventist believers in the Soviet Union. We had a thrilling time of sharing that Sabbath morning.

First there was the music. I don't know when I heard more heartwarming singing than on that Sabbath morning. Then we prayed. I hardly know a word of Russian, but we all spoke the same language that day—the language of love, the language of heaven.

Following our season of prayer together, a dream of nearly five decades came true for me. I had opportunity to step up to a Russian pulpit, open the Word of God, and preach the gospel of our Lord Jesus Christ. And this is what I shared with them:

Thank you so much for your warmhearted welcome, and thank God for making it possible.

Who would have thought the day would come when we would share Sabbath worship like this? Praise to the Lord for His marvelous, miraculous grace.

All of us today should thank God for the love of freedom blossoming in the Soviet Union today. Not since the time of King Cyrus of ancient Persia nearly 2,500 years ago has heaven worked so dramatically through a leader of government. I say again, thank God for President Gorbachev!

And I say that on behalf of American as well as Soviet Christians.

We in the United States deeply appreciate our own President Bush for the way he has worked with your president to foster freedom. Another American president of recent times, John Kennedy, also yearned for freedom everywhere. In the spirit of world peace he came to Europe. And there at the Berlin Wall, before a cheering crowd of thousands, President Kennedy expressed his hope that someday that big wall would come down. Tragically, though, President Kennedy never lived to see his dream fulfilled—an assassination in the city of Dallas, Texas, cut short his life.

Two thousand years ago, another Peacemaker also made a long journey to defy a wall. Our Lord Jesus came to us in the name of freedom to abolish the barrier of sin dividing the human family. He was put to death too. But listen—Christ's death was not a defeat for the cause of freedom as was the death of President Kennedy. No, Christ's death was a glorious victory!

Listen to what He accomplished at the cross: "Now in Christ Jesus you who once were far off have been made near by the blood of Christ. For He Himself is our peace, who has made both one, and has broken down the middle wall of division between us" (Ephesians 2:13, 14).

Jesus achieved through His death what you and I cannot do for ourselves. He became our peace. He broke down the wall between members of God's human family, the barrier sin had erected.

Back when Christ walked this earth, you recall, a wall of hatred and prejudice separated Jews and Gentiles, a racial and religious barrier more imposing than the Berlin Wall used to be. In fact, Gentiles were forbidden on penalty of death from even worshiping with Jews.

THE FALL OF THE WALL 43

Evidence of this death decree was uncovered by archaeologists back in the year 1871. While digging in the ruins of the temple site in Jerusalem, they found the very stone marked with this warning. Listen to the words, translated from both Hebrew and Greek: "No man of another race is to proceed within the partition and enclosing wall about the sanctuary. Anyone arrested there will have himself to blame for the penalty of death which will be imposed as a consequence."

How very sad. At best, Jews treated the Gentiles with aloofness; at worst, they despised them. And the Gentiles responded in the same spirit, regarding Jews as enemies of the human race. Literature of Christ's day seethed with this continuous hostility between the two races.

But Jesus broke through that wall. Refusing to honor national prejudice, He visited Gentile cities and ate at their tables. Then He called His church to gather Jews and Gentiles together into a fellowship of love and life.

Marvelous indeed! But a perplexing question confronts us here.

With all that Christ has done for us, you would expect Christianity—the religion that bears His holy name—to be a model of unity and peace. But no. Church history records incredible conflicts among Christians, battles and heartbreaking persecutions, all in the name of zeal for Christ.

And to our shame and consternation, the situation remains today. Perhaps worse than ever. Think about barriers dividing Christianity. The strife in Northern Ireland, for example. Protestants and Catholics—fellow Christians—bombing and stoning each other. Russia, during the time of the czars, suffered from religious strife, and also in more recent times.

And what about my own country, the United States?

For our first century as a nation, we Americans enslaved black people, fellow brothers and sisters, and some of us even imagined that God approved of it! Even today, a spirit of intolerance lingers in some places. There are invisible walls of prejudice in America between whites and blacks; Anglos, Asians, and Hispanics; Protestants, Jews, and Catholics—walls that keep us from enjoying all that God has for us. How much we need Jesus today to tear down walls of hostility in Christianity, both in the United States and the Soviet Union, and all over the world.

Well, maybe racial or religious prejudice is not a problem in your church—I certainly have not sensed any of that here. But are there other walls, barriers, in your life? In your home? Even our families may be split by walls of hostility and resentment, defiance and suspicion—distrust between husbands and wives, parents and children. Not to mention disputes with in-laws. We might hope that religion would solve these problems. But it hasn't always done that for us.

Why not?

I've thought much about this lately—why do so many Christians fight so much, even in the sacred circle of the family? I'm convinced that the major reason for our problems is that we haven't fully experienced the gospel. We don't understand and accept God's way for us to be saved.

Just what can the gospel do for us? First of all, God's plan of salvation humbles us in the dust. It strips away all human pride and class distinction. Listen: "There is no difference; for all have sinned and fall short of the glory of God" (Romans 3:22, 23).

So there is no difference, no distinction among members of the human family. None of us is better or worse, whether black or white, rich or poor, Soviet or American—

THE FALL OF THE WALL 45

we all were born into the same sorry situation, and even as believers all of us fall short of God's glorious ideal. There is no room for boasting or prejudice.

Never forget it, friend—we are all guilty. And so all of us deserve death. When you hold up my life or your life—or anyone's life—comparing it to Christ's character, we all come up short. We're all equal, do you see? As far as personal goodness is concerned, I'm not OK, and you're not OK, either. But thank God the story doesn't end there. Listen to the good news from the apostle Paul: "God, who is rich in mercy, because of His great love with which He loved us, even when we were dead in trespasses, made us alive together with Christ (by grace you have been saved)" (Ephesians 2:4, 5).

Do you see what has happened now? We have been made alive together in the Lord Jesus Christ. So we're equal again. Before, we were doomed together. But now in Jesus we are redeemed together.

This is such good news it's hard to get hold of. When I accept Jesus as my Saviour, God considers me as perfect as He is. And when you accept Jesus, you are counted that perfect too. We all share Christ's perfection; there is no difference now. When God looks at us, He smiles and says, "These are my beloved children, in whom I am well pleased." This is not because of our great love for God, but rather because of His great love for us.

Do you see how the gospel tears down the walls between us? Without Jesus, we're all the same—lost. And with Him, we're all the same—saved. And it's all by God's rich mercy, His undeserved grace.

So we are all one in Christ Jesus. There's no more need of divisions among us, or comparisons. Comparisons always create barriers of inferiority, hypocrisy, intolerance. Barriers that Jesus tore down at the cross. There is no difference now between believers. We are either saved or lost—there are no second-class Christians. And no special saints who stand more acceptable before God than the poorest struggling believer.

So thank the Lord, friend, you don't have to compare yourself with other Christians. You don't need to prove yourself to anyone—not even to God Himself. He loves you, and He accepts you completely in His Son. Just day by day cast yourself upon His mercy and obey His will. Confess your sins when you fall and claim His all-powerful strength for the next time you face that temptation.

As you continue surrendering your life to Him, He will keep counting you perfect in Jesus. As you rest in His love, He will quietly develop in you a character that will honor Him and make you a blessing to everyone around you.

By His Holy Spirit, God will bring your life into harmony with His holy law of love. He's promised to do it! "This is the covenant that I will make with the house of Israel: 'After those days,' says the Lord, 'I will put My laws in their mind and write them on their hearts; and I will be their God, and they shall be My people' " (Hebrews 8:10).

This experience of character transformation will renew our family relationships. When Father and Mother humble themselves before their children instead of pretending to be perfect, barriers melt. Teenagers finally respect parental authority.

The gospel dismantles walls in our marriages too. One wife testified, "You know, since I stopped trying to judge my husband, and we've both acknowledged our total need of God's mercy, we have a whole new relationship! We never dreamed it would be possible."

Imagine if the whole world would submit to the terms of the gospel. Social and political reforms can only go so far.

We need Jesus to melt the barriers in our hearts. We need our Saviour to unite us to one another and to God.

You might be wondering just how this can happen for you. Please listen carefully. First, confess that you are a sinner, helpless to save yourself. Next, tell your heavenly Father that you believe Jesus came to this earth as your Saviour, and by His saving sacrifice on the cross He paid the full price of your salvation. Finally, open your heart and ask God to accept you as His child because of Jesus.

And you know, when you entrust your life to God through Christ, He writes your name in heaven's book of life. You stand clean before Him, whatever the sins and mistakes of your past. He looks at you as if you've never done anything wrong. In fact, God sees you as perfect, just as if you've always done everything right.

With Jesus as your Saviour, you are adopted by the Father in heaven. He looks at you with a proud smile and says, "This is Vladimir, My beloved son, in whom I am well pleased." "This is Natasha, My beloved daughter, in whom I am well pleased." Not because you are worthy, of course, but because you believe in Jesus.

Does all this sound good to you? It's the gospel, the good news of our salvation.

Upon becoming a child of God, day by day continue opening your heart to God's guidance. He will bring harmony out of confusion and lead you into His special plan for your life. He will transform your character and strengthen you in overcoming temptation. Then one day Jesus will come in the clouds and take you home to live with Him forever.

Well, that is what I shared with my dear comrades in Christ during our unforgettable worship experience. And now may I share a word from my heart with you who are reading these pages?

Where do you personally stand in your relationship with God? Is there a wall between you and your Lord? Do you want that wall to come down so you can be saved? I urge you to entrust your life to Jesus just now.

Chapter 5
Comrades in Christ

It is nothing short of amazing how God has influenced minds and hearts at the height of Soviet power. During my visit to Moscow in September of 1990, I was privileged to meet the honorable Evgeniy Chernitzov, who heads the department for Protestant churches at the Council for Religious Affairs. We talked together in his office at Soviet government headquarters.

Vandeman: Mr. Chernitzov, would you tell us how you feel about the role of Christianity here in the Soviet Union?

Chernitzov: Two years ago, across this country we celebrated the thousand-year anniversary of Russian Christianity. Religion has contributed greatly to our civilization. It united the various tribes and facilitated the spread of our written language and culture.

As for the present situation in our country, we need Christianity's firm moral standards. We also need your help in improving interpersonal relationships in our society. I've noticed that because of the revival of Christianity, the Soviet people have already become more tolerant, more humble, and more kind.

50 COMRADES IN CHRIST

Churches are now quite free to do as they please. Every new day brings more freedom, more opportunities for believers. In the future, I anticipate that they will have the full range of privileges offered by Western society to its believers. In the United States especially we see evidence of what happens when Christians are free to conduct their humanitarian activities.

I've observed that Seventh-day Adventists have led the way in launching these highly noble charitable ventures—even before your church had official permission from our government.

So you see, Christianity has much to offer the development of our nation. The Soviet Union can be compared to poorly cultivated farmland. The Christian church in general, and the Adventist Church in particular, is well suited to enrich the soil of our society in this time of *perestroika.*

Vandeman: Would you tell us more about the new policies promoting religious liberty for all citizens of the Soviet Union?

Chernitzov: For many years we did not have any religious freedom here. The church suffered greatly. Now there is legislation in process that will provide equal rights for believers, for representatives of various confessions without discrimination or favoritism. I think the adoption of this law will indeed provide religious freedom.

Already the Adventists are involved in charitable activities as well as evangelization. They are doing much which even two or three years ago seemed unrealistic. For example, the pastors of the Seventh-day Adventist Church now go to prisons and preach to the prisoners. Your church has received official permission to build a religious publishing house as well as a seminary center. Beyond that, Adventists are preparing to use the mass media to spread your message.

Vandeman: What future developments do you see for Christianity in your nation?

Chernitzov: Opportunities will increase so the church will be able to contribute even more to Soviet society.

Vandeman: Thank you so much for sharing with us today.

So the Seventh-day Adventist Church received special permission from the Soviet government to build a publishing plant for Bibles and Christian literature. But our people here did not have sufficient funds to take advantage of such a thrilling opportunity. That's where our next guest enters the picture—the dedicated businessman from North America who made it possible.

Vandeman: Garwin McNeilus, welcome to "It is Written." You've been a friend of mine for years. What do you manufacture?

McNeilus: We build concrete mixers—the large units that haul the concrete to the construction sites. We also construct the concrete plants and refuse trucks.

Vandeman: And here you are in the Soviet Union, half a world away from your home in Dodge Center, Minnesota. You're here to make an investment. Would you tell us about it?

McNeilus: Well, on my first trip over here two years ago, I could see the intense desire among the Soviet people for Christian reading material. But there simply was nothing available.

Vandeman: What about Bibles?

McNeilus: There's a very desperate need for Bibles. Those who have them share them—people take turns, reading in shifts. I saw that, and my heart went out to the people. I'm here now to do something about that.

Vandeman: Thank God for your investment of one million dollars in the new Bible publishing plant. How is the construction progressing as of this date in early September of 1990?

McNeilus: George, we had the groundbreaking ceremony just this last March. I was out there yesterday. They are putting the roof on the building, and the panels are going up on the sides. The brick for the front portion of the building is in place. There's tremendous activity.

But here's what's really thrilling about this—lay members of the church have come here, living in conditions less than desirable, to build this house of publication so that others might receive the good news.

Vandeman: Now the equipment. Weren't there some providences involved?

McNeilus: There's no question about the Lord's leading. Our giant web press should have cost several million dollars. We found it available for sale over in Scandinavia, complete with printing plates for the Bible in the Russian language. It was sitting there idle and we were able to buy it at a substantial discount. The Lord had it waiting for us.

We bought the press even though we didn't have permission to import it to the Soviet Union. When it came time to move it here, final permission was still not given, but we shipped it anyway. Then we received the good news that the authorities had approved the publishing operation.

Vandeman: Now, this press is capable of producing how many Bibles per year?

McNeilus: Our projection the first year is to produce 1,500,000 Bibles.

Vandeman: A million and a half Bibles! Thank God. People have been smuggling Bibles in and sending them in, sending money for them. To think they can be published right in the country with the government's permission. When will the press be installed?

McNeilus: Plans call for printing to begin in the spring of '91. The press is on the site, stored in the building. But we will start a smaller press in a temporary building within the month.

Vandeman: Now the church here in the Soviet Union doesn't have a great deal of money. Is more money needed to carry forth this Bible project?

McNeilus: Yes. There are tremendous needs remaining.

Vandeman: Garwin, let's talk about what happened with Bud Otis, who coordinates the Seventh-day Adventist work in the Soviet Union with our church's world headquarters. He went to Siberia just a few weeks ago and held a series of meetings. Tell us what happened.

McNeilus: He had quite an experience there, George. They rented one of the major halls in that city, seating 2,000 people. So many people came that they had to hold the services twice a night, 4,000 people a night, crowded into the halls to hear the Word of God. University people came—students, staff, scientists.

Vandeman: They've had no public proclamation of the gospel for seventy years. There's no other word for this surge of interest than hunger. Isn't it wonderful today to help satisfy it? I know a lot of our "It Is Written" friends would like to join you in this project, and they're going to join you in prayer. You have made it very real for us. Thank you so much, Garwin.

Now let's think about another area of gospel outreach close to my heart—media broadcasting. I'm anxious to introduce you to one of the finest young pastors I've ever known. Peter Kulakov lives with his lovely wife, Galina, and two small daughters about a hundred miles south of Moscow.

Vandeman: Peter, welcome to "It Is Written."

Peter K: It's my pleasure to be with you, and welcome to Moscow!

Vandeman: Peter, you're living through a time of exciting change in this great land, a time of reconstruction. How has *perestroika* affected your ministry—your work and your methods of labor?

COMRADES IN CHRIST

Peter K: It's happened so unexpectedly that we were not ready for it, at the beginning. You know, I live in Tula, a city of half a million citizens. Several years ago we had a small congregation of seventy members meeting in a house. But suddenly God provided us a new building, and we now have more than 200 members. We are ready to build a second church.

Vandeman: You and I first met when you visited Thousand Oaks, California, preparing for a thrilling new ministry. Tell us about that, would you?

Peter K: We are preparing radio programs for the Soviet Union. The Adventist Church has permission to build a Christian media center. We already have the ground floor in, and construction is proceeding every day.

And we have another dream. In addition to our media center building, we want to have our own antenna somewhere near Moscow to preach on medium wave radio to cover the European region of the Soviet Union.

Vandeman: Peter, this interview will be seen on television all over the United States, Canada, twenty-two countries in Europe—in fact, over much of the world. What advice would you like to give your friends—spiritual advice, encouragement, and hope for the future?

Peter K: I would ask them to remember that there are millions and millions of people who would cherish the opportunity they have for spiritual food.

Vandeman: God bless you, Peter. We'll be praying for the development of your radio work here in the Soviet Union.

Now, would you like to meet Peter's father? Pastor Mikhail Kulakov leads the Seventh-day Adventist Church in the Soviet Union. He has a remarkable story to share.

Vandeman: Mikhail, I understand that you were in prison in a labor camp under the Stalin regime for a number of years. Would you tell us about that?

Kulakov: I had the privilege to be born in the family of a Seventh-day Adventist minister. My father organized several churches before being arrested in 1946. It was my responsibility to continue the worship services and to continue spreading the gospel. Then I was arrested by Stalin's officers in 1948, along with my older brother.

Both of us were sentenced to five years of labor camp. But the conditions were severe there, and my brother did not survive. But the Lord protected me, and I was able to finish those years of my sentence. Then, upon my release, I was exiled to a remote area of Siberia.

Vandeman: And there you met your wife-to-be—one of the most incredible stories of God's providence I've ever heard.

Kulakov: I didn't realize it, but near the place of my exile was a small group of Adventist believers. Among them was a girl by the name of Anna. And without knowing anything about me or hearing my name, she had a dream. And in that dream she heard my name. The Lord told her that her husband would be Mikhail Kulakov.

A few months later the congregation there got word from our church in Moscow that I had been exiled in the area. They made contact with me—and that's when I met Anna. The first time I saw her I received a deep impression that the Lord had provided me a life companion.

After we got married, Stalin passed away, and I received permission to leave my place of exile.

Vandeman: Incredible! How did Anna feel when she met the man God told her about in her dream?

Kulakov: Oh, she was amazed!

Vandeman: And the Lord gave you six wonderful children—three fine sons and three fine daughters. We just met one of them, Peter. Evidently you have taken sufficient time out of your busy program as leader in the Soviet Union of the Adventist Church to be a good father.

One of your sons, Mikhail, has begun the first Protestant seminary in the Soviet Union in more than seventy years. Along with religious studies he has a unique agricultural training program that has attracted the government's attention. With food so scarce in the country at this time, you are sustaining 200 students, teachers, faculty, and workers at the seminary. They are having all they need because of the work of Dr. Jacob Mittleider. Tell us about that.

Kulakov: At first the authorities were reluctant to allow us to have land. They didn't know what our believers can do. But when they realized the possibilities, they gave us a good piece of land, which we started to develop. It became a center of attraction. Hundreds of people come daily or weekly to see this place and to learn how it was possible to grow large, nitrate-free vegetables in this area.

Not only do we feed our students here from the farm, we also sell excess produce to help support the seminary. And we feel deeply obliged to our dear people in the United

States who helped us get started with this program.

Vandeman: I understand that literally thousands of visitors have visited the seminary to learn the secret of your farm program—including nearly 2,000 government agricultural experts from around the Soviet Union.

Kulakov: The Lord is doing marvelous things in this country. We always expected that the time would come, that somehow the gospel would be preached—but we did not imagine that the doors would open so soon.

Vandeman: Thank God. Mikhail, we could talk on and on by the hour. Thank you so much for taking time from your responsibilities to share with us.

Well, what can we say about what God is doing in this great nation? Thrilling! Miraculous! Words fail us. Who would have imagined all this would be happening, so much, so soon?

Now as we close this chapter, I'm thinking again of that testimony we heard from Mikhail Kulakov, how God provided him a wife during his exile. There's a lot of encouragement in that story for you, wherever you may live. You see, nothing—absolutely nothing—can keep God from meeting your needs, whatever they may be, even in the most hopeless, desperate situation. The Bible says: "My God shall supply all your need according to his riches in glory by Christ Jesus" (Philippians 4:19).

It's through Jesus that God meets our needs. We must entrust ourselves to Christ. Then He can fulfill that glorious promise which means so much to every believing heart: "We know that in all things God works for the good of those who love him, who have been called according to his purpose" (Romans 8:28, NIV).

My friend, reading these pages, do you love God—love Him enough to believe in Jesus Christ and to obey His will for your life? I urge you to entrust your life to Him just now.

Chapter 6
Secret of Fatima

"This is the Holy Father," proclaimed Mikhail Gorbachev, introducing Pope John Paul II to his wife. The Soviet president added solemnly, "We are dealing with the highest religious authority of the world."

Incredible words coming from Communism's most powerful leader.

The beaming pontiff responded, "I'm sure Providence prepared the way for this meeting."

Unbelievable, inconceivable, unprecedented! Can words be found to exaggerate our amazement at this peace conference between two powerful rivals?

Actually, the two men have much in common, as noted by *Newsweek* magazine:

> Both are charismatic world leaders. Both are Slavs. Both were baptized as babies and each studied acting in his youth. Both have risen through hierarchical organizations to positions of enormous international influence. But one is pope, head of the largest church in Christendom; the other is the leader of the Soviet Union, once the world's most militant atheist state.

Their meeting in Rome was the first face-to-face encounter between leaders of the Kremlin and the Vatican. The two men conversed alone in Russian before summoning aides for further discussion. The meeting lasted nearly an hour and a half, and when it was over they announced several agreements. The pontiff placed his blessing on *perestroika,* endorsing President Gorbachev's restructuring of Soviet society. Gorbachev, in turn, welcomed diplomatic relations with the Vatican and raised the possibility of a papal visit to the Soviet Union. The pope hedged on accepting any invitation, perhaps waiting to see if the Kremlin would indeed fulfill its promise of absolute religious liberty.

Just the evening before, President Gorbachev startled reporters by acknowledging his nation's need for religion. "We need spiritual values," he confessed, "we need a revolution of the mind. . . . We have changed our attitude on some matters, such as religion, which admittedly we used to treat in a simplistic manner. . . . Now we not only proceed from the assumption that no one should interfere in matters of the individual conscience, we also say that the moral values that religion embodied for centuries can help in the work of renewal in our country too."

Astonishing words! Some listeners found themselves wondering, Is the Soviet leader Communist?

President Gorbachev's proclamation on the importance of religion set the stage for his meeting with the pope the next day. The two emerged from the papal library behaving like old friends.

Just a year beforehand, few observers of world affairs would have suggested that such a meeting would be possible. The blossoming of democracy and religion in Eastern Europe caught the world by surprise. But you know, millions of Roman Catholics around the world have long been expecting a revival of religious freedom behind the Iron Curtain. Their confidence is based upon something that happened back in 1917 outside the town of Fatima, Portugal.

Three shepherd children were tending their flock around noontime on May 13, a clear day, when suddenly they saw a flash of lightning. Frightened, they turned to flee. Just then they saw the form of a beautiful young woman. This supernatural personage, who later identified herself as the virgin Mary, mother of Christ, claimed to bring a message of profound importance for the Catholic Church. During the span of six appearances to the children, information was disclosed regarding the future of the world and the church.

Have you ever heard about these appearances at Fatima?

Protestants are surprisingly unaware of them and the prophetic importance attributed to them by millions of Catholics. Many books and articles have been written about Fatima, including an Emmy Award–winning film. Some Catholic scholars have actually said that what happened at Fatima is the most significant spiritual event of this century.

Well, what is the message of Fatima? Some of it remains a secret, but here is what is known of what the shepherd children heard. Listen carefully:

> The war [World War I] is going to end. But if people do not cease offending God, a worse war will break out . . . [and God will] punish the world for its crimes by means of war, famine, and persecution of the church and the Holy Father.
>
> If people do not stop offending God, Russia will spread errors throughout the world, and the good will

be martyred. Several nations will be annihilated, but that in the end, Russia will be converted and a certain period of peace will be granted the world.

Then came a special secret for the pope alone. No pontiff has ever revealed it publicly, but insiders at the Vatican privately report that it predicts an awful calamity through which God will work to bring the world to repentance. This might be accompanied by an attempt upon the pope's life.

Well, all this was quite a breathtaking warning for three children to communicate! The supernatural messenger promised to return in the future and clarify the messages. She also instructed the children that five months later, on October 13, she would perform a dramatic public miracle to verify the truth of her messages.

And so it happened. According to numerous newspaper reports, on October 13, 1917, an expectant crowd of 70-80,000 reported seeing a miracle involving a dancing movement of the sun. Whether that actually happened, we don't know. But other elements of the Fatima prophecy have been fulfilled without question. Russia did indeed become a world power, spreading the errors of atheism all around. And there was another terrible world war, worse than the first, just as foretold.

In our generation, the most dramatic event affiliated with Fatima was the attempted assassination of Pope John Paul II. It happened on May 13, 1981—the exact anniversary of the reported appearance at Fatima.

At nineteen minutes past five that afternoon, the little white popemobile was circling St. Peter's Square amid a waving, cheering crowd. Nobody noticed a flight bag being unzipped. Nobody saw the hand reaching inside or the black Browning pistol pulled out.

Sudden gunfire erupted, and the smiling man in white

grimaced in pain. His broad shoulders swayed and slowly collapsed.

Cheers turned to screams. In a dozen languages, the cry of horror rippled through the crowd: "The pope has been shot!"

Bright red blood spurted from a gaping wound. The race for life toward Gemelli Hospital became a scene of deepening horror. Deathly pale and barely conscious, John Paul II murmured, "Why did they do it?"

Obviously somebody wanted to silence the pope. But who?

Evidence suggested that the assassin did not act alone. A trail of evidence linked him to Eastern European Communists. While blame for the shooting was never established beyond question, certainly the motivation was there to silence the greatest threat to international Communism.

Since that assassination attempt on May 13, 1981, the pope has repeatedly commented about it happening on the very anniversary of the Fatima appearance. And on May 13, 1982, one year later, John Paul II made a pilgrimage to Fatima. Surrounded by a crowd of one and a half million celebrants, he thanked the lady of Fatima for preserving his life.

What will happen next? Fatima scholars predict that the dramatic developments between the Kremlin and the Vatican are just the beginning of what is to come. They anticipate more, much more. In fact, they believe that the Soviet Union will actually become a Christian nation.

Before that happens, according to the prophecy of Fatima, the pope must make a specific, public appeal for the conversion of the Soviet Union. After that, the miracle will not be long in coming. This is what millions of Catholic Christians believe will happen very soon.

Well, now we know the message of Fatima. No one can

deny that the prophecy has been strikingly fulfilled so far. But does that prove it came from God? Perhaps those children really saw a supernatural being—but was it really the virgin Mary or an impersonator?

An impersonator! How could that be?

Notice this startling warning: "No wonder! For Satan himself transforms himself into an angel of light" (2 Corinthians 11:14).

Incredible but true—Satan himself masquerades as an angel of light. The same devil that appeared to Jesus as an angel in the wilderness attempts to deceive sincere Christians today—even precious children. The enemy of our souls is cruel beyond comprehension and very cunning.

I don't doubt the sincerity and integrity of anyone who believes the message of Fatima came from God. But a close examination raises some concerns. Back in 1917, even the local parish priest of Fatima at first suggested that the appearance could be a manifestation of satanic power. Was he correct in raising such doubts?

I ask you, Why wouldn't the enemy try to deceive those children—and millions today who receive their testimony as the word of God? Remember, just because something is supernatural doesn't mean it's from God: "Beloved, do not believe every spirit, but test the spirits, whether they are of God; because many false prophets have gone out into the world" (1 John 4:1).

We can't believe every spiritual manifestation—we must test the spirits. And what is the test? God's Word, of course. The teachings of Fatima and everything else we believe must be in harmony with the Holy Bible in order to be from God.

What does the Bible itself teach about end-time events? It foretells a massive religious deception of global proportions involved with a battle called Armageddon. Let's read about it in the book of Revelation:

> They are spirits of demons, performing signs, which go out to the kings of the earth and of the whole world, to gather them to the battle of that great day of God Almighty. . . . And they gathered them together to the place called in Hebrew, Armageddon (Revelation 16:14, 16).

This "battle of that great day of God Almighty" is earth's final conflict. More than human forces will be fighting—the spiritual armies of God and Satan will clash. Armageddon climaxes the Great Controversy between good and evil.

The text said that miracle-working evil spirits will gather together the leaders of the "whole world." This would include the Soviet Union, of course. Evidently, even atheists there will be "gathered together," swept up with the undeniable miracles of satanic agencies. The whole world will be converted to counterfeit worship—all but a faithful few who depend upon the Bible alone for truth.

These are the spiritual issues involved with Armageddon. There may be physical conflict as well.

Where is Armageddon? History offers no record of any place specifically bearing that name, but the Bible offers some hints. Our text says the word *Armageddon* comes from the Hebrew. In that language, the word combines *har*, which means "mountain," and *mageddon*, which many connect with Megiddo. So the name Armageddon can be understood as "mountain of Megiddo."

The mountain of Megiddo—here is a clue we can work with. Back in Old Testament times Megiddo was a small but important fortress city north of Jerusalem near the plain of Esdraelon. Once in Scripture this plain itself is called the Plain of Megiddo.

Recently we took our cameras to Israel in search of Armageddon.

It might appear to be a logical location for warfare, but then we remember that Armageddon involves not a plain but a mountain. We must find a mountain of Megiddo. A mountain with some spiritual significance for the armies of heaven.

Visiting the site of ancient Megiddo might help us understand Armageddon. We drive eastward from the Mediterranean port city of Haifa and follow the Carmel ridge. After passing the northeastern ridge of Carmel we locate the ruins of the ancient city. Looming large over the landscape at Megiddo is Mount Carmel.

Maybe Mount Carmel solves our dilemma. Does it represent Mount Megiddo, the scene of Armageddon? Did something happen at Carmel that could help us understand Armageddon?

Long ago Mount Carmel hosted a dramatic showdown between God and His enemies. The prophet Elijah summoned the nation to appear on the mountain. He challenged them to judge between true and false worship. Listen to his stirring appeal: "How long will you falter between two opinions? If the Lord is God, follow Him; but if Baal, then follow him" (1 Kings 18:21).

God won a great victory that day at Carmel. He defeated the enemies of His covenant, as He will again once and for all at Armageddon.

The New International Commentary on the New Testament explains, "Har-Magedon is symbolic of the final overthrow of all the forces of evil by the might and power of God. . . . God will emerge victorious and take with him all who have placed their faith in him."

So now we understand Armageddon. It's a showdown between truth or error, loyalty to God or to the powers of evil. While there certainly will be devastating battles among the armies of earth, the dominant theme of Scripture is that Armageddon centers around spiritual conflict.

And Armageddon involves every human being personally. To each of us comes the challenge, "How long will you falter between two opinions?"

Yes, all of us have a part to play in Armageddon. When God overcomes the powers of evil, we can overcome with Him!

Let's consider again that message of Fatima. We can certainly appreciate its call to repentance and prayer, but certain other elements of the message raise serious questions. For example, the message of Fatima predicts that after the conversion of Russia a certain period of peace will be granted the world.

We all want peace, but we must beware. The Bible carries a chilling warning: "When they say, 'Peace and safety!' then sudden destruction comes upon them, as labor pains upon a pregnant woman. And they shall not escape" (1 Thessalonians 5:3).

Thank God, we don't have to be caught off guard: "You, brethren, are not in darkness, so that this Day should overtake you as a thief. . . . Therefore let us not sleep, as others do, but let us watch and be sober" (1 Thessalonians 5:4, 6).

One thing is certain. The enemy of our souls knows what he is doing. He has a global strategy for last-day delusions, and he doesn't mind revealing those plans in advance to gain the confidence of millions before plunging them into the depths of deception.

In these solemn times, we must be alert to the final crisis awaiting us before the second coming of Christ: "There shall be a time of trouble, such as never was since there was a nation, even to that time. And at that time your people shall be delivered" (Daniel 12:1).

We find here both bad news and good news. There will be a time of trouble, and we cannot escape it. That's the bad news. But, thank God, He will deliver His committed people. He will bring us safely up to heaven:

> After these things I looked, and behold, a great multitude which no one could number, of all nations, tribes, peoples, and tongues, standing before the throne and before the Lamb, clothed with white robes, with palm branches in their hands, and crying out with a loud voice, saying, "Salvation belongs to our God who sits on the throne, and to the Lamb!". . . Then one of the elders answered, saying to me, "Who are these arrayed in white robes, and where did they come from?" And I said to him, . . . "These are the ones who come out of the great tribulation, and washed their robes and made them white in the blood of the Lamb" (Revelation 7:9-14).

Can you imagine how thrilling that will be! Just picture yourself praising God with the saints of all the ages, a great multitude that no one can number, waving palm branches of victory in Jesus. I want to be among that number, don't you, those who are saved by the blood of the Lord Jesus Christ? Whether or not you realize it, my friend, this moment you are deciding your eternal destiny. I urge you to entrust your life to Jesus and then follow Him with all your heart.

Chapter 7
Defeat of Barbarossa

It happened in the predawn darkness of June 22, 1941. Sudden hell broke loose as Hitler's war machine invaded the Soviet Union. Tanks rolled and soldiers swarmed across the border while bombers of the dreaded *Luftwaffe* screamed overhead.

The bloodiest land battle of history began at 3:30 that fateful June morning. It was a massive blitzkrieg of the Soviet Union, covering a 2,000-mile front from the Baltic states down to the Black Sea. The Germans staged a three-pronged assault. To the north they stormed through Lithuania toward Leningrad. To the south they plowed across the Ukraine toward Stalingrad. Forces in the middle pillaged their way east toward Moscow.

Hitler called his invasion of the Soviet Union Operation Barbarossa after the famed ruler of the Holy Roman empire. The attack caught Stalin unprepared—the Soviets had not expected the Germans to break their secret treaty so suddenly. Armed with the strategic element of surprise, the invaders made startling progress. In eighteen days they advanced 400 miles and captured nearly a third of a million prisoners.

Hitler boasted that his swastika would soon fly over

DEFEAT OF BARBAROSSA 71

Moscow itself. So sure was the *Führer* of imminent victory that he appointed governors in advance to rule over captured territory. He didn't bother equipping his troops for long-term warfare—some units had food for only twenty days. Plans called for the *Wehrmacht* to reach the Volga River before fall, then safely return to warmer winter quarters.

Such was not to be. Within a couple of months the Red Army recovered from the initial shock of Operation Barbarossa. Stalin's stirring speeches mobilized the Soviets in defending their motherland. Meanwhile, German supply lines, stretched beyond measure, failed to adequately sustain the weary warriors on the front lines. Hitler decided to scale down the invasion and focus his forces on a single central offensive against Moscow.

The Germans fought their way to the western suburbs of Moscow, within twenty miles of the city. But they bogged down in a flood of autumn rain that gave way to blinding November blizzards. Then came the big freeze, imprisoning the invaders in brutal subzero temperatures.

On December 6 the Soviets launched a furious counteroffensive that forced back the invaders, crushing the myth of Hitler's invincible *Wehrmacht*. The attackers regrouped for a final charge upon Moscow but failed to get it off.

It was in the north that the Soviets made their most heroic stand. The Germans advanced to within ten miles of Leningrad, meeting heavy resistance from the Red Army. Hitler, wary of the dangers of street fighting, decided to starve the city into surrendering. In staging this siege he underestimated the patriotism of Leningrad's citizens. Even the women and children preferred death to having Hitler's swastika fly over their heads.

Countless thousands indeed did die. Coffins lined the streets. With food rations exhausted, desperate mothers fed grass to their famished children.

Meanwhile, far to the south, Operation Barbarossa resumed with fury. Despite bad weather and courageous resistance, the Germans captured Kiev. The Red Army retreated, not in defeat but to adopt a defense-in-depth strategy. Their maneuver worked. When the Sixth Army of the *Wehrmacht* failed to conquer Stalingrad, the tide of the war began to turn.

Up north, however, Leningrad remained under siege, surrounded on every side. Relief supplies from the United States and Great Britain could not penetrate the suffocating blockade. But then a slender lifeline was opened by the Soviets themselves. Lake Ladoga, northeast of the city, had frozen over for the winter. A convoy of trucks from Siberia crept across the ice unnoticed, sustaining the life of Leningrad.

Finally Soviet troops broke through the blockade and liberated Leningrad. The city had endured incredible suffering. For 890 days, from September 1941 to mid-January 1944, the brave citizens had withstood famine, artillery, and air bombardment. Can you imagine—a siege of nearly 900 days! The toll was terrible. Three quarters of a million had perished, most from starvation or freezing.

But now the winning momentum was with the Allies. As Americans and British swept into Germany from the west, Soviets plowed through from the east. Amid the rubble of Berlin, the Germans surrendered.

The awful war was over. Freedom lovers around the world rejoiced. But peace had come at a fearful price. Of all the nations involved in World War II, the Soviet Union suffered the most, losing more than twenty million soldiers and citizens.

Out of the horror of Leningrad's nightmare comes the thrilling story of Maria Vladimirovna. You can read it in the thought-provoking book *Parting With Illusions* by Vladimir Pozner, the Soviet Union's leading commentator. Pozner met Maria back in the sixties while writing for *Soviet Life* magazine. He saw the plainly dressed elderly woman checking visitors' handbags at the Hermitage museum's Gold Treasure Room.

None of the visitors would have suspected that humble Maria had been born to a Russian nobleman, an admiral in the navy of Czar Nicholas. She spent her childhood years at the Winter Palace, surrounded by the splendor of the Hermitage. After the Bolshevik Revolution, the new Soviet government made a museum out of the Hermitage and appointed Maria as a caretaker. Year after year she faithfully, quietly performed her duty. Then came the day Hitler's invasion interrupted business as usual. All too soon the *Wehrmacht* was pounding on the gates of Leningrad, vowing to exterminate the city.

In that crisis hour the director of the Hermitage museum summoned Maria for a top-secret assignment. "Leningrad may fall," he sadly acknowledged. "We're evacuating our entire collection of paintings and art. But there is something else—the Gold Treasures, the unique works of ancient Greeks . . . they are priceless. I want you to supervise their packing. And once the crates are ready, you will oversee them being loaded onto trucks and have them buried in a secret destination."

Solemnly he charged her: "Maria, you alone will be responsible. Those treasures will be yours until we defeat Hitler and restore them to our beloved city."

Well, that was quite an assignment for Maria. For four long years she lived in a tiny village somewhere in the far north, suffering like everyone else from the cold, hunger, and poverty. Yet at her disposal were millions worth of gold, gems, and other treasures. Who would have noticed the loss of one or two little diamonds out of thousands of them?

But when the glad day came when the Gold Treasures returned to the Hermitage, not one jewel was missing. Maria had been faithful to her trust. And from that day to her death she continued watching over them. The thousands of visitors whose bags she checked never suspected that this humble little woman had preserved for them the national treasures.

Maria is no longer living, but her legacy remains. I don't know if she believed in Jesus—perhaps not. Yet I see in her a symbol of the Soviet church surviving the Stalinist suppression. Christianity was under siege during those decades of darkness. The crown jewels of the faith had to be hidden by Soviet believers. Only God knows how they suffered in preserving the heritage of their faith.

But now, that national treasure is being restored to Soviet society. Once again the name of Jesus is proclaimed throughout this great land. How I thank God for the Soviet leadership that is making freedom of religion possible! And I'm grateful beyond words for the opportunity to bring you this firsthand account.

In these pages we've tried to present in a balanced way the dramatic religious heritage of the Soviet Union. Let's remember that atheistic government was not the only offender in suppressing religion in Russia. In the time of the czars, you recall, the official church itself undermined freedom of conscience.

And Western Christianity has been guilty as well of suppressing freedom of conscience. Any student of history knows that the medieval church massacred millions branded as heretics whose only offense was cherishing a belief in God different from its own.

Should this erosion of faith by the established church surprise us? The book of Revelation foretold the struggles

DEFEAT OF BARBAROSSA   75

of God's people through the Dark Ages. Notice here in Revelation 12, beginning with verses 1 and 2: "A great sign appeared in heaven: a woman clothed with the sun, with the moon under her feet, and on her head a garland of twelve stars. Then being with child, she cried out in labor and in pain to give birth."

Symbolic language, obviously. Who does this woman represent? Well, in the Bible, God often uses the symbol of a woman to represent a church—a pure woman to represent His sincere followers; an immoral woman to represent fallen Christianity. So this pure woman of Revelation 12 must represent God's faithful people. And notice the woman was with child—a child under attack: "Another sign appeared in heaven: behold, a great, fiery red dragon. . . . And the dragon stood before the woman who was ready to give birth, to devour her Child as soon as it was born" (Revelation 12:3, 4).

The dragon here is none other than Satan, mortal enemy of the church. Remember how the devil, working through Herod, the Roman ruler, tried to destroy Christ by murdering all male babies in Bethlehem? But Infant Jesus escaped with His mother, Mary, and Joseph.

You know the story. After Christ grew up and began His ministry, the enemy attacked Him with a new strategy. He approached the Lord in the wilderness with several shrewd temptations. But Jesus refused to compromise His faith.

Enraged, Satan tried yet another tactic. He entrapped the religious leaders with his deceptions. Once he gained control of the religious establishment of that time, the enemy employed the leaders in persecuting Jesus. They apparently conquered Christ at the cross, but He rose victorious from the grave to the throne of God. Notice verse 5: "And she [the church] bore a male Child who was to rule all nations with a rod of iron. And her Child was caught up to God and to His throne."

The devil was thoroughly frustrated in his attacks upon the Son of God. So now he turned upon the woman, the church. He attacked God's people with the identical strategy he had tried against Jesus.

History was repeated in a remarkable way. Listen to what happened. First the devil tried to kill the infant church. He used Roman rulers as his agents, just as he had with Baby Jesus. But despite fierce persecution by Nero and his successors, Christianity survived and thrived. Satan realized he could not destroy God's people by violence alone.

So the enemy approached the church with subtle temptations. He determined to lure its leaders into compromising their faith. Many refused to yield, remaining faithful as their Lord had been when He was tempted. But the enemy did manage once again to manipulate the religious establishment of that day. As in the time of Christ, truth became buried under tradition.

God's faithful people, refusing to participate in apostasy, were put to death, like their Lord had been. History records the tragic story. For many dark centuries, the saints had to go into hiding. We see this in verse 6: "The woman fled into the wilderness, where she had a place prepared by God, that they should feed her there one thousand two hundred and sixty days."

Here we have a time prophecy. A period of persecution—something like a religious Operation Barbarossa—lasting 1260 days. Are these days literal or symbolic? It is helpful to recall that the book of Revelation deals in symbols. Remember, too, that the persecution lasted many centuries—much longer than 1260 actual days. It was more like 1260 years. Is this the time frame indi-

DEFEAT OF BARBAROSSA 77

cated by the prophecy—1260 years?

That is what the reformers taught. Martin Luther and his fellow reformers taught that this prophecy represents 1260 years of oppression by the church of the Middle Ages. Space in this chapter does not permit me to explain his reasoning, but I urge you to read my book *Showdown at Armageddon*, available from the publisher of this book. Chapter titles include "Antichrist's Civil War," "Secret of the Rapture," and "Counterfeiting Armageddon."

Do you see another symbol here reminding us of Maria Vladimirovna, heroine of Leningrad? Just as she preserved the national treasure during the dark years of the siege, so the church of the wilderness preserved the jewels of truth during the dark centuries of medieval persecution.

God did not forsake His people in their wilderness exile. Revelation 12 verse 16 says that "the earth helped the woman." The mountains of the Alps and other remote places of the earth provided refuge from total extermination. The light of truth never went out completely, though it burned quite dim.

Reformers rose up, one by one, to bring back truth that had been neglected during the long centuries in the wilderness. Martin Luther appeared on the scene to restore the gospel, the heartbeat of Christianity. And the Reformation began—but it was not finished by Luther in the sixteenth century. Light had only begun to break forth in the wilderness tunnel.

Notice this from the book of Proverbs, chapter 4:18: "The path of the just is like the shining sun, that shines ever brighter unto the perfect day."

Truth, if we follow it, will shine brighter and brighter. Ever more glorious. Always advancing. Never retreating. Never standing still. Can we see now what God is attempting to do with His people? He wants to preserve every ray of light each Reformer so carefully guarded, revealing newly discovered truth that also had been lost through the centuries. You see, just as the hidden treasures of the Hermitage were restored to Leningrad after the long siege, God will restore His jewels of truth. After long centuries of darkness, they will shine forth in all their beauty just before the coming of Christ.

We see this final restoration of truth described in the last verse of Revelation 12: "The dragon [Satan] was enraged with the woman [the church], and he went to make war with the rest of her offspring, who keep the commandments of God and have the testimony of Jesus Christ" (verse 17).

We have here a description of God's last-day people. Did you notice their twin identifying marks? Keeping the commandments of God and holding to the testimony of Jesus. Evidently faith in Christ and keeping God's commandments go together.

I urge you to study this carefully. Find out for yourself what it means to keep the commandments of God—all ten of them, in a spirit of faith in Jesus.

Think about that day when our Lord Jesus Christ breaks through the eastern sky. Think about it over and over. Let it give you something to live for. Could anything be more exciting to contemplate?

Seeing first a small black cloud. Watching it move nearer and nearer till it becomes white and glorious. A cloud like none you've ever seen before—a cloud of angels, uncounted angels. Hearing a sound like none you've ever heard before—the sound of a trumpet echoing round the world. Then a voice like none you've heard before. It's the voice of our Lord calling the dead to life.

The earth quivers. Tombs burst open. Angels everywhere carry little children to their parents' eager arms.

Loved ones long separated by death reunite with shouts of joy, never to part again!

What a reunion day!

As the resurrected saints are drawn upward to meet Jesus, we who have been living join them in the air. Imagine the feeling! Defying gravity, we soar through the sky. Without a space suit we sail through the stars up to our heavenly home.

And when we get there, what a welcome! Angels crowding about us, singing songs of praise to God. We will sit down to a homecoming banquet better than any dinner ever enjoyed on earth. And best of all, the heavenly Father Himself will introduce us to our paradise home.

What a home it will be! Mansions—what will they be like? Certainly more glorious than the richest dwellings on earth. I can hardly wait to see them, can you? Even more, I can hardly wait to see the Lord Himself, our heavenly King!

I want to be there, and I know you do too! God help us be ready for that great day.